BRAIDING STARLIGHT

Susan Deer Cloud

SPLIT OAK PRESS

2010

BRAIDING STARLIGHT

Poems by **Susan Deer Cloud**

Split Oak Press

ISBN: 978-0-9827521-6-6

FIRST EDITION

Split Oak Press

P.O. Box 700

Vestal, NY 13851

splitoakpress.com

ACKNOWLEDGEMENTS:

Some of these poems have been published in *American Indian Culture and Research Journal*; *Florida Review*; *Yellow Medicine Review: a Journal of Indigenous Literature, Art & Thought*; *Paterson Literary Review*; *The Broome Review, a Journal of Contemporary Literature*; *Sentence: a Journal of Prose Poetics*; *Blood Lotus & Il Circio*.

"I Hate Emily & Sylvia aka NDN *Ars Poetica*" received an Honorable Mention in 2007 Allen Ginsberg Poetry Competition.

Cover art by Dorothy Little Sparrow Watson

Cover Design by 30 Editing and Design

CONTENTS

Braiding Starlight is dedicated to

John Gunther
who loves mountains

*

my beloved Aunt Pat and Uncle Lou Johnson

**

my beautiful poet brothers, Rane Arroyo and Glenn Sheldon

***

In memoriam for Sweet Rane
who braided the starlight with me

Long Time Ago (for Lance Henson)

Long time ago invisible in the woods
wolves ran alongside us.

Long time ago unseen panthers purred along
night branches, gold eyes many Grandmother moons
lighting our path.

Long ago before the wolves
were trapped in a gauntlet and clubbed.

Long ago before the great cats were shot
into extinction.

I have heard it said long time ago
our hearts greeted strangers like mountain roses
fully opened.

I have heard it told we really did know
Indian love medicine, touch

so tender it made us cry tears in shapes
of blue deer and brave eagles.

Brother in poetry, long time ago
we learned how to condole each other
when our hearts closed,

re-open our ears, eyes, throats.

Oh, my brother, I am so afraid.

The wolves. The panthers. Our moon flowered hearts.
Long time ago, long time ago.

Kindergarten Revolutionary (for Black Bear)

Unlike you sent to
Indian boarding school,
the State forced me when four
into public school across
our street. I told you
before kindergarten my life
flowered free in forest behind
stuccoed house Grandfather built
on the borderland. When teacher
ordered us to nap on Army cots,
I pulled blanket of yellow
like a tipi over limbs and head ~
beneath yellow my fingers
playing cowboys-and-Indians
and the Indians always won.
The other children fell asleep~
and every school day after
a children's garden of faces
budded shut. Maybe they are
the ones still obeying, still sleeping.
Perhaps those who never flowered
to freedom became the reason
for the metastasized poor
in desolate ghettos and
desperado mountain places ~
for imperial wars, crashing
markets, clashing hates.
Are they now the ones
manipulating everyone
to shut eyes, mouths, hearts,
while I stay awake,
fingers conjuring visions
of justice with NDN red pen?
Friend, you suggested I write
a poem about that first day
of kindergarten

and the mixed blood girl
staring between two worlds.
I smiled "Yellow has always
been my favorite color."
I never added you remind me
of my Indian grandfather
who gave me the blanket
of yellow.

Only Jewish Indian Girl in America

In 50's Catskills called *The Borscht Belt*
because of Jewish hotels still in their grandeur,
I thought I must be America's only living
Indian girl who was also "part Jewish."
Father seldom mentioned his jeweled "blood"
just as Mother spoke little about being Indian.
Maybe if we remained quiet, genocide
would gallop away like a Cossack
on a horse. Besides, we simply *were*.

Once my father drove us to visit a lady
who survived Auschwitz. We perched
smiling in rocking chairs on her veranda,
chatted about her cat and morning glories,
Heavenly Blue. I would not have believed
the fire-haired woman who gave us
Jewish honey cakes and fresh farm milk
had nearly starved in a concentration camp
had I not glimpsed her wrist, tattooed
numbers reminding me of the inky zeroes
inside some Indian elders' eyes.

Occasionally at sunrise I walked
to our town's synagogue, sneaked
behind walls of stucco mixed
with glass shards glinting like stars.
I knelt to pick up fallen sparkles
more splendid than bought jewels,
in the psalm of my hands broken
rainbows like all the people of the world,
all the world's *kristallnachts*,
gathering the fallen together
to flame from my palms
like a prayer.

Poetry Mom

What we learned when it was too late ~
we'd been sterilized.

What was that saying they thought witty?

Nits make lice?

The efficient doctors strode
in, saw to it.

Who wants more Indian babies?

A Mohawk friend told me
ancestors aborted themselves
during French and Indian Wars.

Or made certain they didn't get pregnant

in this misery of stolen land, every day
wounds and disease breeding more corpses.

Or staggered mad in blue moon snow for hours.

Or committed suicide with blades, shotguns, firewater.

And still do.

Every day crying for my seed that was stopped

while *The Air-Conditioned Nightmare's* mothers
boast about being hockey moms, soccer moms.

Convention's *Drill, Baby, drill!*

Earth, Dreamer Mother, I know how it feels

when they drill yet another hole in you.

Fist (for Paul Hapenny)

"So it happened,/ with no visible violence, with honey/ and words, I was broken." Rafael Alberti

I.

All their university friends advocated non-violence.
Also, they were against sexism and racism.
Not one went in for homophobia.
So when he pulled her long Indian hair,
yanked her into whiplash pain and years
of tranquilizers, she watched numbly
while the friends gazed away, staying
peaceful. When she appeared like
a concentration camp victim
from the esophagitis the pain brought,
body burning to holes from the inside out,
she nodded at friends who oozed she had lost
a lot of weight as if it were a good thing,
"You can never be too rich or too thin."

II.

And when, fashionably thin, she divorced him,
and their friends who were really his friends
didn't question his lies or ask if she could survive,
she reminded herself that educated people
must always act civilized. Wasn't that
what the professors in Germany did when
one by one the SS dragged off Jews, the Gays,
the Catholics of Conscience who taught
by their sides? Here in America
they have Indians and others like her
to practice their civility on.

III.

She often jokes that her new friends,
kind pacifists and vegans of course,
are more evolved than her. Perhaps
they don't have daylight nightmares.
She still wants to scream when she sees
her head bent to an angle, bones nearly sticking
through her skin. When you feel what it's like
not to be able to lift your face to the stars
or dream beauty because your bones jab
into the bed and back in at your insides,
it is possible you might question turning
your other cheek again and again.

IV.

You I have no word to call by ~
Friend? Brother? Something deeper, more?
I need to write this after you spoke about predators
so cold, so murderous, they kneel to nothing but the fist.
Maybe a strange gratitude *this*, yet I thank you for not
violating me with any sucrose of lies sweetening
me into the silent burials of "civilized." Warrior,
I tell you I wish that woman had had your decent fist
to borrow all those years ago. Hard to write this even now,
but I know your heart will recognize its *rough*
fighting to heal the hurt tongue.

Thank you, *nia:wen*, for giving me a dream, the stars.

Baggage

It is your birthday and I am thinking
of the October day my lawyer told me
I'd have to sue my husband "on grounds
of cruel and inhuman treatment." I stood
looking brave, until I stumbled out the door.
"I loved him once," I whimpered to a cynical
shrug. I ran to the elevator, blinded by final
tears for that betrayed love.

Next I got treated to all the clichés
one suffers during a divorce, including
the saw about having too much baggage.
I always hated that cliché most ~
the safe people's smug pretense
of wisdom when they remind you
life gets harder once you have all
that baggage. How could anyone
love such a baglady?

I was never smart in their way.
I knew what they meant,
but in my crazy poet's wisdom
I imagined the accumulations
of pain and sorrow and also joy
would become my poetry over time.
It is your birthday and I am thinking
of last night when we had what you
call a fight. No, it was our baggage
hungering to become our poetry.

I woke 3:30 in the morning.
Still half-asleep, I started crying.
Just a little. I don't cry much anymore.
Streetlights seeped through my shut
red blinds and appeared like bars across

8

my body. Me all locked in. I heard you
growl again, "Don't retreat over this. Don't.
I love you." I still have the old knapsack
from when I traveled light. I sewed gold braid
and lucky shamrocks on it. For your birthday gift
maybe I'll take up my old knapsack.

Globe

Then there is the white man who
wants to live with you. When you ask,
"Have you *really* thought about
how it would be to live with an Indian?,"
he embraces Blake's "Exuberance is beauty" ~
"To live with you would be Heaven!"
Next he sends a poem about his boyhood
and the globe that comes out of a box
each Christmas. How did he know
if he wrote you a foolhardy
love poem about a snow globe
he'd at last turn you upside down,
break your shields into tiny glistenings
like the sole night such a globe shone
under a Christmas tree for you,
a girl fleeting as snow crystals?
On Christmas Eves you still wonder
what happened to your magical world.
Then his poem. Then being
unwrapped.

My Grandmother Dreams of a White Christmas
at Irving Berlin's House

~ and this story a hand-me-down from
my Aunt Pat, as much as the 12 K gold locket
she once bequeathed to me, my Indian grandfather's
teenaged face so handsome inside its filigree heart
I even fell in love with him a little ~

~ as much as my first ice-skates,
oversized hockeys handed down to me
by my cousin, Jimmy, as much as
torn long johns passed on
by an older brother so I wouldn't shiver
too much when I skated and tried to fly

until the tears next to my skin might feel holy ~

~ like the polka dot dress
I still wear in the sole studio photograph
taken of me, my brothers and baby sister,
the summery dress my mother bought
for ten cents at a rummage sale
because her daughter thought circles
beautiful ~

and wasn't it a bargain, my long dress
of many colored circles kissing my bare
legs with each step ~

~ yes, this hand-me-down story returning
as autumn revolves into winter solstice,
when "I'm dreaming of a White Christmas"
yearns once more through TVs, radios,
mall loudspeakers and Facebook postings ~

~ Aunt Pat describing
my auburn haired grandmother
working at Irving Berlin's Catskill home,
washing floors and China and dusting off
his piano where sometimes he sang "White Christmas" ~

~ grandmother who never lost
her Irish freckles when the winters whitened,
whose skin glistened as white snow fell
and kept on falling as snow would do
during World War II ~

~ every morning my grandfather
drove my grandmother to Berlin's
Turnwood house painted as snow,
glimmering like elusive purity
on the other side of Shin Creek,
behind high fence whose wood allowed
glimpses between a million slats
into a magical life ~

~ each sunset my stone mason grandfather
picked up my grandmother in his blue Ford
with the running boards, both of them
wearied down to Empty
and traveling the dirt roads back ~

~ in those ration days when sleigh bells
no longer jingled along horses' rippling flanks,
no gaiety of tossed mane or exuberant snort,
only my freckled grandmother who had lost
her mother and favorite brother, Everett,
who played his fiddle at dances the same
as their red-haired father did, also dead ~

~ and here Aunt Pat's voice always tightens,
"Uncle Everett was killed at the Battle of the Bulge,
all they sent my grandmother was his violin" ~

~ my aunt's hand-me-down story
making me stumble as those thick-bladed
hockey skates made me trip when I sliced them
across river ice, second hand tears making me
feel like falling snow covering over
the story of my grandmother at Irving's house ~

~ and in my falling I hear the Jewish immigrant
sing in a distant room while my grandmother dreams
of days she "used to know," while my mother
is carrying my oldest brother, and my father
is being shot on a Pacific island right as I'm dreaming
my spirit here ~

~ O Mr. Wonderful Irving Berlin, did you ever
get a clear glimpse of my grief-skinned grandmother,
gentle lady who made your mountain house
so bright ~

Bone Glows (for Brian Broadrose & Family)

The autumn my mother lay dying
in distant hospital from breast cancer
invading bones

she cried for us to carry her back
to mountains that first grew
girl bones like delicate blades

of starlight. Four a.m.,
sleepless, I am her age
that winter she died

back in our Catskills.
Colonials don't seem to know
why Indians wish their bones

and ancestors' bones
to glow silence forever
in the land they rose from.

Why is it our job to keep
explaining? I am listening
pre-dawn to the April stars,

to the first bones of mystery,
hearing spring beauties and violets
moving to blossom above my mother.

Why must I explain what it means
to have had a mother who cradled me
in our woodlands of wildflowers?

I hear tears of stolen ancestors
whose bones became numbers in boxes,
research in the reservations of basements.

14

I hear how they've cried from prying white fingers.
In the last of night I pray with first bird song ~
One day may my bones dream with my mother's.

Changing the Language of Conquest

That dusk after we walked
to New York woodlands falls,
photographing each other
so that we might slip
the day into some solid memory
we could touch in a future loneliness
as we touched fingers to each others'
faces when dusk bruised into night,
your face in passing headlights
flashing into fractals of yearning,
you making it clear as Venus
you desired me, hours after
we left March snow melting
in end of winter light, body shadows
writhing black across white
starting to show ancient seabed ~
that day, that dusk, that night
when I brushed curve of
index finger beneath your blind
eye, quarter moon of flesh
milkweed silken as a child's skin,
that moment, that infinity,
when my touch winced
at knowing you had been dragged
by Myanmar thugs to Insein Prison,
kicked and whipped to unconsciousness
just as your closest comrade
was tortured then hanged,
night when I wanted the stars
to dangle over us and twinkle
and convince us there's a Heaven,
but we shivered at town edge,
only lights McDonald's,
Pizza Hut's and Denny's,
that evening groping in your car's
back seat as if two teenagers

16

in love, just like that golden oldie song,
as if neither of us ever had
a man's fist beat the dream shit
out of us, blind the sweetness in us,
you copping a feel between my thighs
after that day we vowed
would be our special day
because before prison you majored
in geology at Rangoon University,
because we two born in 1950
on Earth's opposite halves
love stones, fossils, minerals, seashells,
and when you kissed me
as though I were a Burmese dish
whose spices you hadn't tasted
since you began your exile
I recalled a Cree friend
saying I should read a book
called "something like"
Changing the Language of Conquest,
"I will read it," I thought
in an old dumb grief
as you flung still black hair
back and closed your eyes,
the seeing and the unseeing,
moan of rapture split
by a river of pain,
that artificially lit night
when I collected your face
in my hands, in my trembling,
fluent in stone.

You Are Driving North in November

After sunset
you are driving north
to Canandaigua
nothing but CD music
to keep you company
car heater
warming your legs
in dark stockings
while past windows
starless cold
cornfield stubble
a missed cornstalk
like a lone Indian staff
dead leaves
for eagle feathers
at field edges
trees like shadows
loom upright
in passing headlights
like corpses
the real shadows
you think
of flag-draped coffins
from Iraq
Afghanistan
not shown on TV
from another war
Crosby, Stills, Nash
& Young sing "Helpless"
car taillights ahead
red trails
floating over
old Indian paths
buried ancestors
"Helpless, Helpless"
you blink back tears

trying not to crash
into the twisting
shadows   trying
to make a treaty
with this beautiful
loneliness

Sweats

I've never been to a sweat. Yes, *that* kind, ones people
ask me about because they've read up on us, learned
that Native Americans "do sweats," cry out *Mitake Oyasin*
when water hits hot stone ~ because everyone knows
we all speak Lakota at such times, emerge
from our steam womb into a sublime world
wrapped in a shawl of stars.

Nope, I've never gone to a sweat. But when I almost
embarrassedly admit this, New Agers, wannabes, and
other unabashed annoying two-leggeds don't hesitate
to brag about those thousand sweats they've sweated
in, how cleansed they felt staggering out,
how "the ceremony" got them in touch with their
Inner Honest Injun, with the "Raven Stars" and "Red Wolfs"
that their memories recovered by renegade shrinks
tell them they are reincarnated from.

"You really oughta go to a sweat someday," they pity me.

Yep, poor pitiful me who's never sweated, unless
you want to count my "younger day" forays
to health spas, hunched among "sisters" crying
for a vision of model thin flesh. Or perhaps
my current night sweats and hot flashings
could pass as mobile sweat lodges.

I've never been to a sweat. With all due respect
to Indian traditions everywhere and even to those
New Agers, wannabes, and other hallucinators
who are really only hungering for their original faces
that once waited inside Mother Earth, I suspect
something so fierce in me, so *steamed*
that my people had the old ways
stolen from them, that

I don't want to sweat, pray, risk dancing out
into starlight, the product of some beautiful
ethnic cleansing, blue lie, that any Indian heart
can ever blaze sweet and trusting again.

All my relations, the world is cold.
All my relations, I can't shed
my shawl of tears.

Ode to O Holy Nights in Liberty, New York

Discharged from the Air Force, your poet cousin
flew home. You ran away from University
to rejoin the Universe. Kent State shootings were past,
Vietnam War wasn't. Daisies the Flower Children planted
in gun barrels failed to seed peace. You had chanted
"1 2 3 4, we don't want your fuckin' war," dodging
tear gas on D.C. streets instead of smelling the Catskill roses.
You got a job typing for Liberty Community Action Center,
signed letters to Representative Hamilton Fish, Jr. ~
Peace & Love, Love & Kisses, RED POWER.
Your cousin and trickster-you rented an apartment
above Goody's Bar & Grill, ninety bucks a month ~ split
rent, bought some youthful freedom. He said "cool"
to your occupying the large front room with high
windows laced by wood diamonds across upper panes.
You grinned "groovy," bought a waterbed and gold
silk India spread embroidered with peacocks.
That bed got pretty damned cold in colder weather,
dreamed other cocks would be its heating element.
Your cousin and you tossed socks and underwear
in upside down wampum purple umbrella dangling
from ceiling lamp cord, first sight to greet people
when they blew in through the open door.
Back then, visitors appeared like sweet winds ~
but in the 21st century this gets harder to explain.
You rescued a black kitten with panther eyes
from the alleyway, named her "Cocaine"
after a Dave Van Ronk song. You and your cousin
dined on berries, tamari-splashed brown rice,
Brie on baguettes, washed simplicity down
with peppermint tea ~ every meal a picnic
brightening your bare floor. You felt so Rimbaud,
so Baudelaire. You washed tea down with Bordeaux
the tint of garnets. Neon sign under windows blinked on
and off until sunrise, flashed scarlet electrons over walls,

ceiling, fragile skins of anyone who graced your room.
Friends sat in a tribal circle and didn't "Bogart that joint."
Ike shot smack up in windowless bathroom, skin-
popped a few other hungering freaks. Jimmy,
cousin's oldest friend, died last year of Hep-C.
"Closer to me than my own brothers," your cousin's
voice squeezed through a thousand miles of phone wire.
We didn't cry. We had gotten used to it.
You listened to silence, remembering
two Indian boys "playing Indian"
during the McCarthy years. Tommy died
of Aids in San Francisco, where he retreated
to escape small town hatred. After 9/11
Ike became a right wing flag waver, only thing
left for him to wave. You missed the decade
when he was nodding off. Sammy, paralyzed
in a teenage diving accident, died in 1975
from lung failure. But in 1971 Liberty, long-haired
men bore his wheelchair up sagging stairs, parked him
like a king under that poster you found one rainy dawn
in a muddy gutter: WAR IS NOT HEALTHY
FOR CHILDREN AND OTHER LIVING THINGS.
When Sammy dropped acid, he believed he danced.
A paraplegic dancing on Owsley Orange Sunshine~
Man, that to us was more fuckin' beautiful
than Jesus walking on the sparkling waters.
Next, Jimmy would hallucinate into a shaman
with trickster hair black as Raven's feathers,
rainbows flickering in its flying strands.
The hippie women smiled mellow yellow
in granny dresses flowering down to
patchouli-anointed feet which kicked away
all shoes, boots and any bra-burner bullshit
yelling "Men are sexist pigs!" "Just most
of you are," they'd toke and joke, joyfully
braless from the time they sprouted tits.
"Burn what bra?" Off and on
like the nights' neon, everybody bounced
and balled on the sloshing waterbed.

Except Sammy, of course, who was dancing
with the peacock sun. He had a crush
on green-eyed Lucy who slashed her artist's
wrists when Disco discolored life to polyester.
We played flutes, guitars, blues harps.
Your cousin, spouting naked poetry
and flapping his skinny arms,
became a rebirth of Thunderbird.
We sang, giggled madly, couldn't stop
laughing our rapture and absurdity.
Nor did we suspect in Liberty's holy red light
that made every lover look Indian ~
an American winter was descending
to bury us, little by little,
in big white lies.

Scratch-Offs
(for Erelene, Michelle, Rich & Karin)

March. I slug on at minus zero.
Five days to April Fools. Isn't it the way
of every year? Arctic lows, then flame
buds leap to leaf, daffodils alchemize air
to gold? Won't May's apple blossoms tinge
snow despair with rose? I would fling
myself into sureness of life circling
back to grab at my dead heart, but

for now I don't dream at this border dividing
the city's poorest and richest, crack dealers
and legal drug dispensers, cracked
window houses and mansions with a view.
I drive to mountains I grew up in,
seventy miles of freedom on 17 East. Maybe
for one weekend I can forget the wars
and gas prices shooting so high I fear
I'll be stuck forever in this gash of city,

yes, smile among trees, rivers, lakes, eagles,
rumors the panthers aren't really extinct, will
return with spring. For three months I've wished
to celebrate my sister's birthday. Only now
do I and others gather after blizzards, sleets,
black ice of freeze moons. One gift I bring
are scratch-offs, as she did for my birthday ~
briefly a little girl hoping I'd win big.
My turn to watch her with tiny dime scratch

to the numbers, but, damn, no million dollars,
no thousand a week for life, just thirty bucks.
"Hey, I'll treat us to brunch tomorrow," she grins ~
then her tears. "People like us never win.
We work hard until we die from hardship.
Christ, I'm tired." Soon we are drinking.
Drink until our fears soften. Rage.

25

And my sister, friends, and I sparkle like
Catskill brooks about *what we will do when we win~*
form a tribe, live in woods, play our music,
paint dreams, dream poetry, be the anti-War,

stop buying "people like us"
are America's scratch-offs.

The Road of Dead Dogs (for Ronny Guijs)

….. We are speaking over the phone about Indians. Of course, any talk about my people leads to roads and reservations. So soon our friendship words weave together memories of out West ….. New Mexico, Arizona, Utah ….. you from the Netherlands, me a mountain Métis from Catskills, separate memories shape-shifting into single Navaho rug. I drift on your Amsterdam accent, faraway bells, silver skates ringing across ice, winter canal songs balm for ears hurt by American noise. Somewhere in there I admit I'm tired, yearn to take Indian body of me like red she-fox into deep woods, curl up, let fur and bones of this spirit die noiselessly into earth. *Oh, Ronny*, I yet breathe, *there are times when Chief Joseph stands at my shoulder, when I hear his defeat* ….. *"I will fight no more forever."* You echo me, my brother, echo Joseph, complete the desolate chief's words for me ….. *"From where the sun now sets, I will fight no more forever."* At that moment you *are* Joseph, sad proud warrior who understands his people, women. How grateful I am for this kindness in a land made lonely, my Turtle Island …..

….. You speak of reservations, driving through them ….
Navaho, Hopi, Apache ….. Arizona road you can't forget, light flashing up, millions of smashed stars from the shoulders. *Then I saw* ….. you hesitate ….. *realized I was being blinded by the million broken bottles of a million broken Indian hearts.* Only that way you describe the dazzling light makes brokenness strangely beautiful. I become your bedazzled girl with no memory of soldiers …… path ahead soft spangles ….. no compulsion to slash girl wrists with trails of glass. You lead me to another road, one between Santa Fe and Abiquii. *So many dead dogs and coyotes I named it The Road of Dead Dogs*, your voice drops into a ditch of death. *And along the highway a restaurant, Road Kill Café, YOU KILL IT, WE'LL GRILL IT on sign.* Of course, any conversation about Indians, shattered glass and dog corpses leads to why America is lost. *Why is the richest country on earth slitting her wrists with shards of glass grief?*

27

Why does my Turtle Island drown in blood? Why are the hearts of its women on the ground? .....

..... Mid-winter. Moon a tossed bottle cap. I wane, emptied bottle. Hands lacking heart lines reach to toss me away. *Me* ..... old enough to consider how in former days I would have made love to you, a much younger man, eyes bluer than my NDN blues. How I would have wrapped you warm in my shawl of skin that those soldiers you make me forget would have sold for bounty. And the worth of a "squaw"? Fifteen silver shillings for a killer to get shit-face on whiskey with. Yes, you and I tell each other our loneliness, about living far from home ..... when we go back it is changed, nearly nightmare. Ronny, my brother, my cousin, my friend, once I could have guided you to a land of panthers unscarred by roads. Now my days are as Chief Joseph's nights, a new breed of bounty hunters hunts skins like mine. As we hang up you lilt *Sweet dreams*, strand of lullaby in tender warrior's voice. On this sub-zero night, *farewell* is all I have to sleep with ..... and the million broken bottles of a million broken Indian hearts .....

This Poem Is Not for Revising

anymore than you and I are for revising.
This poem is being written past midnight
to Blues playing on Friday night radio.
This poem is so goddamn blue the font is black,
my soul in one of its Black Irish/Blackfoot moods.

This is a poem not for revising
because this poem is an honest poem that howls
for you and me to "get down" and make love
the way love gets made in a real fine blues song,
sax, sex, sweat and whispers moaning to screams.

This poem refuses to revise, its root is in
the heart, the cunt, the cock, the simultaneous *come,*
is being written to the Blues the way you and I
are being written to the Blues, Babe, alchemizing
into rhapsodic odes to the naked body.

This poem is not for revising because you
and your Blues Mama blaze inside each other
where craft doesn't exist, only naked poetry.
This poem won't get an A, will never graduate,
professors will hate it because it has no theory.

This poem is staying rough to Blues on the radio,
to the urban night violet with mist after rain
playing the Blues along the empty streets.
This poem is not for revising because it craves you
unrevised, tender/raw/real/funky and crying
your Blues-eyed beauty into its dusky arms.

I Hate Emily & Sylvia aka NDN *Ars Poetica*

I was sitting Indian-style on the floor at an Amherst Books
poetry reading. I knew it would be one of *those readings*
like a New England funeral when the first poet, a young man,
stated, "I must apologize before I start. My first poem
is a little political." So I was stuck in the crowd's web
of designer jeans, thinking, "Great. But why are you
apologizing? Honey, you're young. You're supposed to be
political." I listened to his poem mirroring one of those
picture puzzles where you get to find the hidden animals.
I just couldn't find the political animal in his poem.
Abandoning the hunt, I noticed that books on nearby shelves
were remainders. Cool. Really cheap books. I eased out
Charles Bukowski's *Slouching Toward Nirvana*, leafing
through it, waiting for my friends to read so I could slouch
out of there. I decided to buy Bukowski's posthumously
published book, revel in it in the long hot bath I'd partake of
back at my latest temporary place. I was imagining my aching
bones from sitting two and one half hours, three minutes and ten
seconds on hard dirty floor, drinking Pabst Blue Ribbon Beer
because drinking crappy beer seemed to be the "thing"
at these Friday readings.

Driving home I had to go past Emily Dickinson's house,
and I thought of wings and hope and all that shit. I flew on by,
driving six hopeless miles of back roads to where I live with
the trees. Once inside I poured myself a glass of Bailey's
Irish Crème Liquor. I was in one of my black Irish-Indian
moods but still kind of happy from the crappy beer.
Next I ran the bathwater full blast, dumping a mad mix
of mandarin orange and coconut scented bubble bath into
churning H20. It was starting to snow outside and that put me
in a tropical mood. I lit candles, shimmied and slipped out of
my soft skirt and velvet blouse and flowered stockings and
red suede boots ~ just me, a female Gaugin, and Bukowski,
lolling naked together in the balmy bubbles. So I'm reading
about Hank's escapades in Long Beach, getting drunk in bars,

fucking hookers, cursing out women, punching men, having
young girls crawl through his window once he was famous
enough for them to think his pockmarked face perfect.
I'm reading this stuff and playing with myself a little,

only I'm getting too pissed off to go all the way. I keep
remembering how Emily Dickinson was one of the few
women poets taught to me when I was in school. Her
and Sylvia Plath. *Our woman poet role models.* Emily
who spent her adult life inside safe rooms baking cookies,
making tight cold poems, while Walt was wandering the land,
all expansive and ragged and sprouting hair and beard like
sweetgrass. Emily, who never got laid or made love or smelled
a man's sweat mingling with hers in such a way she'd feel
wildflowers bursting out through the star pores of her parasol-
shaded skin. Emily. Poet my male friends prefer because
her poetry is spare. How about poetry fat, nasty, revolutionary,
raw, rowdy the way we women really prefer to be? And Sylvia.
Feminists bemoaning Sylvia plunking her head in a turned on
gas oven after imagining her model self a Jew somewhere in
between Daddy and Ted Hughes. I wonder what she would have
done if she grew up an Indian girl? I ask why no one praises
any women poets for doing what Bukowski did? What would
Hank have done if he'd been in Sylvia's shoes? Left the kids
with Hughes, gone dancing barefoot in a pub with a poet lover
fifteen years younger than Ted and ten times better in bed? I sip
more of what I call goddess milk, smiling at bubbles crackling
in an exquisite water music, sparkling in rainbows ephemeral
as spontaneous song. I'm thinking of my own escapades,
how I earned my reputation of Native American Jezebel,

but, hell, that's in the city I escaped from, where during
the Burning Times the Puritan types would have torched me
as a witch instead of torturing me on the rack of behind-the-back
gossip. Ah, the tropics, me and Bukowski slouching toward
nirvana. When do I get to be praised for having beautiful
young boys crawl through my window to make love with me?
When will I get admired for drinking, brawling, balling, and
growling words like *fuck, bitch, shit* to sound tough? When

31

do I get respect for wandering the land with sweetgrass hair
and wearing no underwear under my outer clothes? I want
to know why the Dickinson house docent thought it wonderful
that Emily lowered cookies from her virginal bedroom
to neighborhood boys waiting below. Who the fuck cares?
I, for one, would think it more wonderful if she had lowered
a ladder for the boys to climb up. Where is the female poetry
that doesn't wear a corset or chastity belt, or involve a vaginal
oven? Where is our American Lalla, our poetess who sings
her poetry naked while whirling into ecstasy?

Yeah, me and Bukowski word-fucking in the tropics
on a snowy night six miles from Emily's house, nothing inside
my oven, coming together in a bubble bath, reaching nirvana.

Smith Handshake

She was hired to convince alumnae
to donate money to lure minorities
into Smith College. Only her supervisor
said she didn't shake hands properly.

She had to learn the Smith handshake.

"Yeah?" I asked. "What's that like?"

She recited, "It's a small
hug. Take the other person's hand,
hold it a little, not too much. No
nonsense. Press. Release."

She demonstrated the quick
touch like snail's slime.

I suppose they hired her
because she's a *Native American,*
a Métis like me who falls under
the *exotic* category. Mirroring
the Land 'o Lakes Butter Squaw
has been a big selling point for us.

Never mind our brilliance.

I drove back to the woods, drew out
my tobacco pouch, offered thanks
for growing up with less "opportunity"
than younger Indians.

Bad enough I earned University degrees,
read more books than I can remember.
But I never learned anything like the Smith handshake.

I never learned to fuck that way, either.

The Personal Is Political

They were on Google Chat,
both entering their 8th decade
(think "Growing old
ain't for sissies").
He said last night
he popped a whole
Oxycodone for his
arthritic knees. Surprise ~
he got the munchies,
first time in over
forty years. He ate
an entire box
of chocolate cupcakes
from Piggly Wiggly ~
bloated, chugged down
a gallon of milk.
Tongue orange
from icing,
he floated out
on Neptune Beach,
languorously
smoked a cigarette
as if he just had
stellar sex.
That reminded him
he wanted
to have sex with her,
the rest being X-rated.
So she typed
her legs especially
longed to spread
like eagle wings for him
in a secret meadow
(sometimes even she
can barely believe

how she kisses
the blarney stone
of her own tongue).
He lapped it up
like goddess milk,
promised her
they would roll in clover
when the apple trees
pinked to blossom.
He typed, "After, can we
have cupcakes and drink milk?"
She wrote, "Of course. But
I'm curious. How do you feel
about eating carrots and broccoli?"
He wrote, "Carrots and broccoli
are the enemies of the people. LOL."
She type-giggled back, "Lololololol."
For post coital Chat they liberated
their proletariat cupcakes
from solitary confinement.

Indian Men Friends Call
(for Monty, Paul, Black Bear & Kris)

Indian men friends call in the middle of
Pinot Noir nights, at sunrise or while I am teaching ~
and because I forget to do what I ask students to do,
turn off the cellie, I hear the music of my friends
inviting me to jingle dance and wave *Laterz*
to smirking students who I can see
wouldn't mind soaring like eagles
through hard-edged windows up to
a blue prayer of sky.

Monty, Cayuga man, calls
mostly at three in the morning,
enough that my Indian name for him
is Three in the Morning Man ~
and when he calls he is usually prowling
the needle-and-condom strewn streets
of ghetto Rochester, cursing the "pigs"
as we yearn for the old free days and he says
Susan, it is time the Cayugas were given the land back,
but the only country we have are these poets voices
winging invisibly from one starless city to another
to the screams of sirens. Monty ~ who reads me
poems grown in sidewalk cracks
and shattered glass.

Paul, Métis man, calls
on ultimate Indian time, which means
whenever he feels like it and often
when he is driving a rented car 80 mph
to some L.A. meeting about his latest film,
or he's out past Boston,
or maybe just landing in Nova Scotia
or Vancouver. It is as if his house
hardly exists, even though I have mailed
visions to his address. He mocks all

small souls who would steal our freedom ~
teases me, speaks in a voice whose music
is of the waters flaming over
and rounding river stones in Catskills
I come from ~ white pine voice
in green breezes, poetry tinged
with midnight snow.

Black Bear, Blackfeet-Cree man,
like other Indian men friends
always calling on the move ~
telling me of the latest pot
he is shaping from Kentucky clay
where he now lives, and I hear
the patient homesick hands
of the past in his telling –
he who likes to phone at nine a.m.,
laughing "Hey, Shine, y'up, yet?"
~ Laughs more when I mutter
"I'm talkin' to you, aren't I?
You just wait until I drink my coffee!"
Bear who has a gift for calling after
Three in the Morning Man hangs up
at dawn. Who went to the Indian
boarding school that never could steal
Montana Holy Dogs galloping through
voice recovered from red earth.

And there is Kris, Diné Man,
calling from Navaho country or
texting me pics of a purple butte
and yellow mountain at sundown ~
another poet and also traditional farmer ~
warrior making a stand
to preserve Black Mesa and all
Beauty Way lands ~ phoned once
while feeding the goats with his father,
and I wished I were there and could
hold a little goat in my arms,

37

or cradle a newborn lamb, or leap up
on one of the horses Kris moves among,
even though I am a disgrace when it comes
to the riding of horses, butt and thighs
purpled like buttes the few times I rode.

Indian men friends call ~
Monty, Paul, Black Bear, Kris, others ~
and, damn, I love those dreamer men
for their nomad mad glad talk
braided with Indian time laughter
keeping me awake.

Native American Wisdom

Every so often people ask me
for my Native American wisdom.
First I stand there, silent.
Possibly I am remembering
all the times I've been a fool,
having a flashback to
a William Blake quip ~
"The road of excess leads
to the Palace of Wisdom."
But the sky-eyed seekers see
my silence as smoke-signaling
my Native American wisdom.
Once this silent noble Indian
stops toking on holy memories,
I breathe dramatically, lifting
two arms up like eagle wings.
I soar, "You have your own
native wisdom. Simply fly
far down into your heart
and all your whirling atoms.
It's right there."

Often I flap my wings happily
because I am thinking about
the firefly night a cousin flew
his van off a bridge, us in it,
too drunk and exuberant to die ~
or the Yuletide my sister sped
over parkway meridian Yield sign
and kept right on driving as if
we lived in a cartoon, "Thwap!"
and nothing could ever touch
us and our laughing.
"Oh," I add to those who hunger,
"if anyone charges you big bucks
for their traditional wisdom,

39

that is known as Native American
fakery." Then I come in
for a landing, ask
if they'd care to barter
twenty bucks for my poetry book.

Waking to Rain, I Think of You

I woke to rain this morning after weeks
of riptide heat burning through sea
of humidity, my cat and I each day
and every night feeling like oil-covered
baby turtles they keep displaying on latest
bad news about Gulf of Mexico BP oil spill.
"Wretched," my sister gave it one word
as we half drowned, sick and weak.

But this morning July air cooled
and one of the first songs a man
sang to me, "In the Early Mornin' Rain,"
drifted in among raindrops. And
the other song, "The First Time
Ever I Saw Your Face" ~
memories sliding down slender
silver streamings past window screen.

And there is a magnificent tree a couple
of lawns away. I have lingered in bed
during all seasons feeling that tree speak
to me in its tree language, and we are
always happy together. This morning
I thought of your love for the red trees
of the north coast, and how you are tall
and make me feel you are as much tree as man.

Once after lovemaking, my first husband
said during a thunder-rumbling dawn,
"There is no happiness greater than lovers
listening to rain after sex." This morning
I woke thinking of you and how we have
not made love and the way I miss the love
we never made. The rain stopped.
In the tree many invisible birds sang.

Dog Boy

swaggered into class, slouched
behind graffiti-gouged desk ~
Fuck You, ripped hearts, *Rap Rules*.
Eyes spat green fire from back row,
shoulders hunched in "rebel
without a cause" nonchalance.
I could have called him Karma
for I wasn't too old to forget
being sent to school counselor,
me and my wooden Indian mask.
"Teachers say you have an attitude,"
counselor sneered. "A *bad* attitude."
I stared ~ inside me a graffiti heart.

I never told that nineteen year old male
he reminded me of my younger self.
My wolf clan eyes leaped
through his cockiness, no flinch
of fear. Him with ADD
and Mick nose no longer able
to smell the wild roses, too much
coke up it. But some days
I drove home to bleak apartment,
tears rolling over high cheekbones
while car wheels rolled to fate
rolling her dice all crazy.

Maybe, dear reader, you think this
will be one of those "To Sir, With Love"
stories. It could be, a little.
In uplifting ending I would gush
about the memoir Karma wrote ~
thirty pages at a college where students
are not expected to write more than ten.
Instead, I'll share how he seethed in class

about his stepfather beating him,
how he never let that bastard see tears.

I raced out onto the lawn of night,
wiggling through doghouse door
where I held my dog tight and sobbed
my way to sleep and slept til dawn.

I gave him an A+ for that and his paper.
Dog Boy told me I was the best teacher
he ever had. I don't know where
my Karma went to with that A
and the plus looking like a cross.
Please, where do the beautiful
beaten children go to?

I danced out on the wildflowered
night with dog turned to wolf
born of tear-stained stars.

The Girl (for Barbara Mann)

The girl whirls back
into sight, a hologram
there yet not there, and

should your hand at last
steal the boldness
it lacked in 50s' Catskills,

fingers flutter toward
the girl's sunburned fingers ~
what might they touch

besides an elusiveness
of light? In your child's
shyness, you didn't understand

how to speak to the girl.
You only shadowed
her shine when she swirled

barefoot across summer fields,
hair black whirlwind
kissing her back. Her hands

collected stones, roots, berries,
blue eggs and golden feathers.
Her dog, which people mumbled

was really a wolf,
also silvered after her.
The girl who gathered spirits

drew non-spirit voices from gossips ~
She's a loony, witch, slut.
Even though you were barely

six, you sensed the older girl
was lonely. Your mother
whispered *The girl comes*

from Canada, knows medicine,
is Mohawk like you. Her wolf
even licked your hand once.

Home Calling
(for Paula Gunn Allen)

Lately New Mexico calls to me.
Maybe it's the friends, maybe mesas or
some purity of light that never left
my heart when I waved *Vaya con Dios*
to Taos. I still see that young woman
blaze like dawn along canyon walls,
believing warmth will soften any
hardness. She comes as a stranger now,
her face in mirrors rock, no sun
touching the shadow places
with holy fire.

Here in the East I've grown too sad,
eyes clouded with falling towers
on a stolen island ~

here, after you died in the night, Paula,
I recalled winter's conversation,
you lilting *Lately New Mexico calls to me*
in 1940's gin & cigarette voice, lung cancer
and chemo further roughening the mix.
Certainly we spoke about mixings,
two *mixed bloods*, *breeds*, yearning
for home, some steady earth balancing
our feet. And I'll carry forever

understandings you gifted to me
from north California beach ~
Many mixed bloods, especially
women, feel chronic fatigue.
The "bloods" war against each other
inside our bodies. My Scots-Laguna
mother taught me that. We half-
laughed about others failing to notice

our terrible tiredness. You joked *Yeah,*
they think we're normal, never suspect
we're about to faint, or worse, we're poets.

Lately friends urge me to write happy poems
and odes of joy call to me as New Mexico calls ~
then, Paula, I remember your death song,
Despite the cancer, despite my house
burning to the ground, I won't give up.
I'll grow stronger. I'll dance again
at Laguna Pueblo.

New Mexico called you all the way, Paula.
In my grief I dance with you, your beloved
trumpet vines in bloom, hummingbirds whirring
deep into orange flowerings of happiness, you
a pain-free girl blossomed with bird energy.
Sparkle-eyed daughter of dawn, I hear you ~
laughter of last stars, dreams of turquoise,
sage-fragrant limbs flying, shining.

Paula, it's over, the split life, the wars inside
and out, the human cruelties, stupidities.
Sister to so many of us, welcome home.

At This Hour

At this hour edging into first morning
the street glimmers even quieter than forest.

How free of cricket chirps my third floor ~
my writing garret, next to it garret with bed.

And although still August, tonight's sunset
leafed out in autumn's frayed reds.

All of this evokes ancient poems
painted by Japanese ladies of the court.

I even wear scarlet kimono from Japan
a wayfaring poet friend brought home for me.

Soon the haikus of my hands will cease writing ~
silk cranes flying across thighs.

Soon this yearning must lie down where your body
felt like wings turning me to sky.

(for John Gunther, my hiking companion)

Jackknife

I.

This evening on Florence Ave
I lifted my face to quarter moon
and star beneath it.

October air a cool kiss ~
something about living alone,
all the universe becomes one's lover.

Shivering beneath streetlamp ~
remembering University days
when I packed a jackknife
inside my long skirts.

I told you about it,

how I carried pearl-handled knife
and tense body across Endicott's
ghost town streets and back lots,

dispelling elongated shadows of my fear
after riding night bus with the Bird Lady
and Cat Lady tweeting and meowing,

told you my gay cousin borrowed
the knife after an evening's binge
in hometown Blueroom, our favorite bar ~

I need it for protection, he begged it from me.

I had heard those who hissed *Faggot*
at him. Same rednecks who sneered *Cunt*
when they didn't *get any* from me.
In our Catskill town you can imagine

how often *Cunt* surprised my inner ear
like night blooming cereus, because

I chose to hear it as compliment, a flower,
so I'd always walk in the garden.

II.

That Dog Day night my cousin lost my knife
between staggering off into muggy heat
and passing out on his parents' lawn.

Today you told me *You don't really understand.*
what it is to be gay. Not really.

What it's like to be kicked out
at seventeen by one's Puerto Rican father
because you love men —

beaten by a Papi others call Spic ~

to walk out each day fearing some stranger
will murder you because you were born
to love in this way.

I never bought another knife, despite
terrors whose causes might shock
even you I still keep secrets from.

Day after my cousin dropped my weapon
in some ditch or mud puddle, we laughed about

the vision of him or me poking a puny blade
into some Indian-hating homophobe used to gutting
bucks and smashing rabbit skulls on rocks ~

Sure, we can take down any retro-Neanderthal.

My cousin and I loved each other back then,
in the forever summer days when we shared our poetry.

We decided to booze it up in the Blueroom again, grow
brave to the jukebox tune of Hank, Patsy, Dolly,Willie.

I think that was the quarter moon we did a war dance
on the pool table.

Braiding Starlight (for Rane Arroyo)

At the meeting of two Indian-named rivers I wept my goodbye
Your ear glistened into dying cell phone a thousand miles distant

After you died I dreamed of birds clustering around me
Birds vivid colors of tulips, the red kind your favorite flower

May's moon whirls closer to Strawberry Moon
Now wherever I wander I wear a shawl of bright birds

All day soft and musical it rained like your voice
All day Persian cat purred as she used to whenever you sang

Following spring rain night rivers rise drunk and howling
Friend, Beloved, this sorrow is braiding starlight